SCOOBY-DOO!

A SCIENCE OF FORCES AND MOTION MYSTERY

By Megan Cooley Peterson   illustrated by Dario Brizuela

THE ROGUE ROBOT

CAPSTONE PRESS
a capstone imprint

A cool breeze flittered off the ocean as the gang dug for clams.

"I can't wait to eat these clams," Shaggy said. "Too bad Funland hasn't opened for the summer yet. I bet they'll have all sorts of groovy snacks."

"Funland looks a little spooky," Velma said.

"Maybe even haunted," Daphne added.

"Geez, Scoob. *Clam* down!" Shaggy joked.

Scooby pointed toward the amusement park. "Rhost!" he shouted.

"Ghost?" Shaggy, Velma, and Daphne said together.

"This calls for an investigation, gang!" Fred said.

"Everything's running, but no one is here!" Fred exclaimed.

"A robot is riding the coaster. How is that possible?" Daphne asked.

"It could be gravity," Velma said. "It's a force that keeps the coaster in motion once it starts."

"Like, what's a force?" Shaggy asked.

"A force is a push or a pull," Velma explained. "Forces cause motion."

"Which means gravity pulled the coaster down the first hill," Daphne said. "But how did it get *up* the hill?"

"I'm too hungry to solve any mysteries," Shaggy said. "Let's check out that hot dog stand, Scoob."

FACT FILE

Sir Isaac Newton (1642—1727) was a scientist, astronomer, and mathematician. He studied motion. Over time he came up with ideas about how and why objects move. Newton's ideas became known as the Three Laws of Motion.

"Anybody there? Can we get some service, please?" Shaggy called. "We'll have a plate of hot dogs to go with all the fixings."

"Rum!" Scooby said, licking his lips.

6

"Scoob, please tell me you pushed that plate of hot dogs," Shaggy said.

"Rot re," Scooby said, shaking his head.

"Hot dog ghosts!" Shaggy yelled.

"Does a force always cause movement?" Shaggy asked. "Because those hot dogs, like, moved all by themselves."

"Something moved those hot dogs," Daphne said. "But a force doesn't always cause a motion. Forces can cancel each other, and then the objects stay still."

DOWNWARD FORCE

UPWARD FORCE

"Shaggy and Scooby exert a downward force on the bench," Velma explained. "The bench exerts the same upward force on them."

"Otherwise the bench would move?" Shaggy asked.

"You got it," Velma said.

"Rhew!" said Scooby.

HOT
DOGS

FACT FILE

Forces and motion are always at work, even when you're asleep. The Earth revolves around the sun and spins on its axis. Depending on where you live, you may be moving around Earth's axis faster than a jet airplane!

"I could sit here forever," Shaggy said. "This bench is, like, totally comfy."

"You've just described inertia!" Velma said.

"Like, *gesundheit*!" Shaggy said.

"No, inertia," Velma said. "It describes how an object at rest tends to stay at rest, unless acted upon by a force. That's Newton's First Law of Motion."

"The same is true of moving objects," Fred added. "Objects in motion tend to stay in motion."

"That means Shaggy will stay on the bench until a force moves him," Velma said.

"Or that robot!" Daphne cried.

"Ret's ro!" Scooby shouted, pushing Shaggy off the bench.

"Come on, Scoob. Pick up that robot's scent," Shaggy said.

"Ro rent," Scooby said.

"No scent?" Shaggy asked. "Maybe it was a ghost. I guess ghosts don't leave a scent."

"Rhost?" Scooby asked.

Shaggy pointed to the Hall of Mirrors. "There he goes, Scoob! Let's follow that robo-ghost!"

"Man, look what those hot dogs did to me," Shaggy joked. "I'm stuffed!"

"Re roo," Scooby said.

"Zoinks! The robot!" Shaggy cried. "Let's get out of here!"

"What are you doing?" Daphne asked.

"Like, that robot is totally after us," Shaggy said. "But look how strong we are! He doesn't stand a chance when I try to throw him!"

"Not so fast," Velma said. "An object's speed gets faster or slower based on its mass and the forces acting upon it. That's Newton's Second Law of Motion."

"Those toys don't have much mass," Fred explained. "No offense, guys, but it doesn't take a lot of force to move them."

GAME
BOOTH

FACT FILE

Mass and weight are different. Mass is the amount of material in an object. Weight is a measure of gravity's pull on an object.

"Try to throw this bowling ball with the same amount of force as with the toy," Velma instructed.

"I can barely move it!" Shaggy exclaimed.

"That's right," Velma said. "The bowling ball has more mass than those beach balls. You must use a stronger force to accelerate it the same amount."

"Which means you won't be able to throw that heavy robot," Daphne added.

"Let's find the park's caretakers," Fred suggested. "We'll get to the bottom of this."

"Are you the caretakers of Funland?" Daphne asked.

"Yes. I'm Mr. Jenkins, and this is my sister, Sarah."

"All the rides in the park are running," Fred said.

"And the lights are, like, totally on!" added Shaggy.

"The rides aren't running," Mr. Jenkins said. "And we would have seen the lights."

"The moonlight played tricks on your eyes. You kids run along home," Sarah said.

"We're not done investigating, gang," Fred said back at the park.

"The taffy machine is totally haywire," Shaggy said.

"And who turned on the lights and rides again?" Daphne asked.

Scooby pointed toward the Tunnel of Love. "Rook!" he shouted.

"The robot! He's going into that ride," Fred said. "Let's follow him!"

TUNNEL
OF
LOVE

"Zoinks!" Shaggy shouted. "The robot sent his raft flying! He must have magic powers."

"Not exactly. Forces come in pairs," Velma said. "For every action, there is an equal and opposite reaction. And that is Newton's Third Law of Motion."

"She's right," Fred said. "The robot jumped off his raft. That's the action. Then the raft moved in the opposite direction. That's the reaction."

"Look! He's getting away!" Daphne cried.

"Like, I think your driver's license has expired. Your driving is crazy!" Shaggy shouted at Velma.

"The steering and the brakes don't work," Velma said. "I can't control the car!"

"Ruh, roh!" Scooby said.

"I'll drive through that pile of taffy. Maybe friction will slow us down," Velma suggested.

"Holy smokes, it worked!" Shaggy exclaimed. "But how?"

"The car's wheels rubbed against the ground and the sticky taffy," Velma explained. "Friction is a kind of force. It slowed down the car."

"Do you hear footsteps?" Velma asked.

"The robo-ghost!" Shaggy shouted.

"Mr. Jenkins? Fred asked. "What are you doing here?"

"I'm here for Charlie, my robot. I built him to run the park. But it seems he went a little crazy."

"You can say that again," Shaggy muttered.

"Could you kids help me catch him?" Mr. Jenkins asked.

"We're on the case!" Fred said. "We can use that magnet to pull the robot toward us."

"Like, how?" Shaggy asked.

"With magnetic force," Velma explained. "You can't see it. It's invisible, just like gravity."

"That's right," said Daphne. "A magnetic force can push or pull a magnetic object without touching it."

MAGNET GAME

"My device says Charlie is close by," Mr. Jenkins said. "Point the magnet toward the hot dog stand."

"Zoinks! The magnet is working," Shaggy said.

"I'm afraid my robot has seen better days," Mr. Jenkins said.

"Somebody must have really pushed his buttons!" joked Shaggy.

Scooby pointed toward a menacing shadow. "Rook!" he shouted.

"Who's there?" Mr. Jenkins called out.

"Sarah? What's going on?" Mr. Jenkins asked.

"What's going on?" she huffed. "You and that silly robot! I knew I couldn't convince you it was unsafe around children unless I proved it to you. I re-programmed Charlie to show you what could happen."

"You sure showed him," Daphne said. "That robot went totally bonkers!"

"Now that this mystery is solved, Scoob and I will volunteer to eat up—I mean clean up—all that taffy," Shaggy said. "I'm so hungry I could, like, eat a robot!"

GLOSSARY

accelerate (ak-SEL-uh-rayt)—to increase the speed of a moving object

axis (AK-sis)—straight line around which an object rotates

force (FORS)—any action that changes the movement of an object

friction (FRIK-shuhn)—a force created when two objects rub together; friction slows down objects

gravity (GRAV-uh-tee)—a force that pulls objects together; gravity pulls objects down toward the center of Earth

inertia (in-UR-shuh)—the tendency of an object to remain either at rest or in motion unless affected by an outside force

magnetic (mag-NET-ik)—having the attractive properties of a magnet

mass (MASS)—the amount of material in an object

reaction (ree-AK-shuhn)—an action in response to something that happens

SCIENCE AND ENGINEERING PRACTICES

1. Asking questions (for science) and defining problems (for engineering)

2. Developing and using models

3. Planning and carrying out investigations

4. Analyzing and interpreting data

5. Using mathematics and computational thinking

6. Constructing explanations (for science) and designing solutions (for engineering)

7. Engaging in argument from evidence

8. Obtaining, evaluating, and communicating information

Next Generation Science Standards

READ MORE

Biskup, Agnieszka. *Super Cool Forces and Motion Activities with Max Axiom.* Science and Engineering Activity. North Mankato, Minn.: Capstone Press, 2015.

Weakland, Mark. *Thud!: Wile E. Coyote Experiments with Forces and Motion.* Physical Science Genius. North Mankato, Minn.: Capstone Press, 2014.

Winterberg, Jenna. *Balanced and Unbalanced Forces.* Huntington Beach, Calif.: Teacher Created Materials, 2015.

INTERNET SITES

FactHound offers a safe, fun way to find Internet sites related to this book. All of the sites on FactHound have been researched by our staff.

Here's all you do:

Visit *www.facthound.com*

Type in this code: 9781515725909

Super-cool stuff!

Check out projects, games and lots more at **www.capstonekids.com**

INDEX

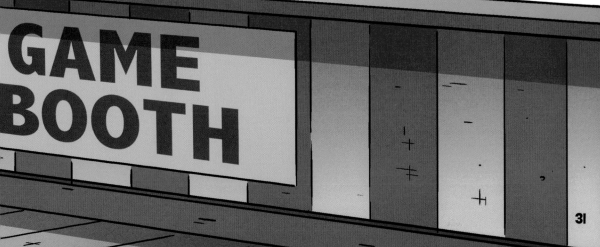

GAME
BOOTH

Thanks to our adviser for his expertise, research, and advice:
Paul Ohmann, PhD, Associate Professor of Physics
University of St. Thomas, St. Paul, Minnesota

Published in 2016 by Capstone Press, A Capstone Imprint
1710 Roe Crest Drive, North Mankato, Minnesota 56003
www.mycapstone.com

Library of Congress Cataloging-in-Publication Data
Names: Peterson, Megan Cooley, author.
Title: Scooby-Doo! a science of forces and motion mystery : the rogue robot /
by Megan Cooley Peterson.
Other titles: Science of forces and motion mystery
Description: North Mankato, Minnesota : Capstone Press, a Capstone imprint,
[2016] | 2016 | Series: Scooby-Doo!. Scooby-Doo solves it with S.T.E.M. |
Includes bibliographical references and index. |
Audience: ages 9-12. | Audience: grades 4 to 6.
Identifiers: LCCN 2015043265 | ISBN 9781515725909 (library binding) | ISBN 9781515726517 (ebook
PDF) Subjects: LCSH: Force and energy—Juvenile literature. | Motion—Juvenile
literature. | Scooby-Doo (Fictitious character)—Juvenile literature.
Classification: LCC QC73.4 .P463 2017 | DDC 531/.11—dc23
LC record available at http://lccn.loc.gov/2015043265

Editor: Kristen Mohn
Designer: Ashlee Suker
Creative Director: Nathan Gassman
Production Specialist: Gene Bentdahl
The illustrations in this book were created digitally.

Printed in the United States of America.
032016   009681F16

OTHER TITLES IN THIS SET:

A SCIENCE OF ENERGY MYSTERY

A SCIENCE OF SOUND MYSTERY

A STATES OF MATTER MYSTERY

Clay County Public Library

116 Guffey Street
Celina, TN 38551
(931) 243-3442